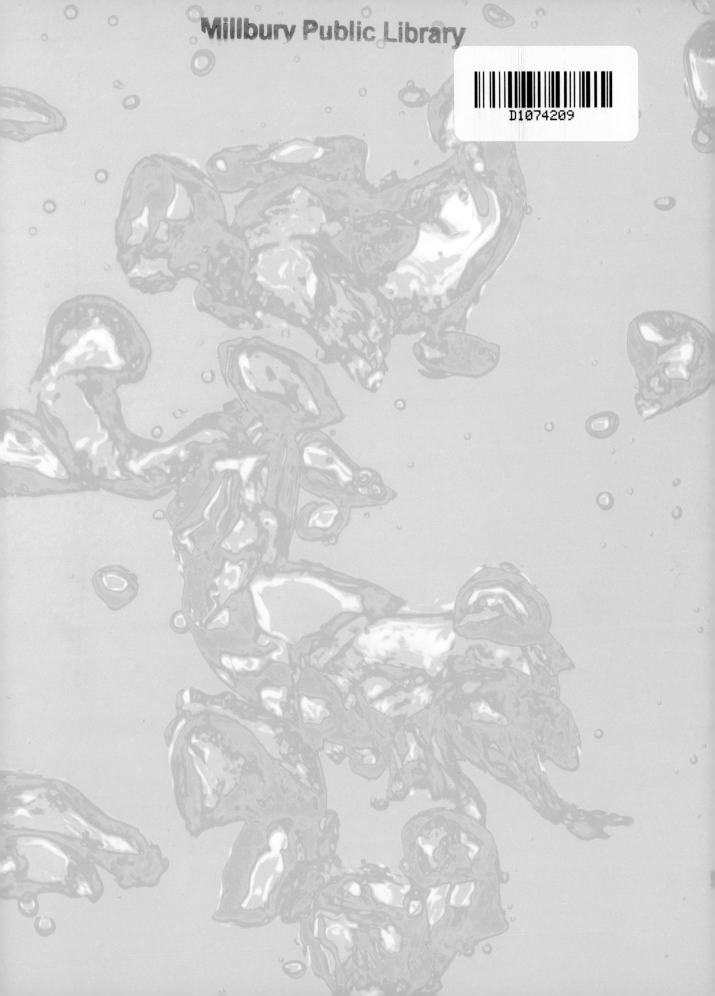

Flooding and Drought

LOOKING AT LANDSCAPES

Flooding and Drought

Clive Gifford

A+
Smart Apple Media

First published in 2005 by Evans Brothers Limited
2A Portman Mansions, Chiltern Street
London W1U 6NR

Consultant: Simon Ross, Editor: Sonya Newland, Designer: Big Blu Ltd.,
Picture Researcher: Julia Bird

Published in the United States by Smart Apple Media
2140 Howard Drive West, North Mankato, Minnesota 56003

Library of Congress Cataloging-in-Publication Data

Gifford, Clive.
Flooding and drought / by Clive Gifford.
p. cm. — (Looking at landscapes)
Includes bibliographical references and index.
ISBN 1-58340-732-4
1. Floods—Juvenile literature. 2. Droughts—Juvenile literature. I. Title. II. Series.

QB1399.G54 2005
363.34'93—dc22   2005040510

9 8 7 6 5 4 3 2 1

Contents

Introduction

Water is essential to life on Earth; all living things need it to survive and flourish. Water is the main constituent of living matter—between 50 and 90 percent of the weight of all living organisms, from microscopic bacteria to giant blue whales, is water. On Earth, water exists in all three states of matter: as a solid in the form of ice, as a liquid in the forms of freshwater and seawater, and as a gas in the form of water vapor.

There is a vast amount of water on the planet, but its distribution is varied. Many regions have plenty of water, while others have very little. Too much water or too little water are two of the world's most serious natural hazards.

A flood occurs when a body of water rises and overflows onto normally dry land. Floods can

▲ From space, Earth is a mass of blue—oceans make up 70 percent of its surface.

▼ Droughts—long periods without rainfall—combined with human factors, such as the use of water for agriculture, can cause lakes, rivers, and even inland seas to dry up completely. This barren area in Australia was once a lake.

bring benefits to local populations, such as helping to create fertile farming soil, but they can also bring destruction and misery to human settlements. Floods can wash away crops

▲ In some parts of the world, floods can create fertile land for farming. Here, farmers in Burma plow a rice field on a floodplain.

and valuable soil and cause landslides or mudslides that engulf villages and cause destruction to property and even loss of life. They can also damage or destroy infrastructures such as transportation and communication links, making rescue attempts extremely difficult. Floods can damage sewage and other waste-disposal systems, which means that water supplies can become contaminated, greatly increasing the threat of disease.

Droughts may not be as quick, dramatic, or spectacular as the raging torrents of water produced by some floods, but they are equally—if not more—devastating. Droughts are long periods in which a region experiences an abnormally low level of rainfall, or no rain at all. This is the most serious physical hazard to agriculture in nearly every part of the world. It can cause soil to dry out, plants and crops to die, and streams, lakes, and rivers to dry up. At its worst, drought can result in widespread famine and death for thousands of people.

Water on the Move

Water is on the move in rivers, oceans, the ground, and high in the atmosphere. The movement of water is one of several factors that can influence climate and weather conditions that, in turn, are a major cause of floods and droughts. Climate describes the average weather conditions experienced by a particular area over a certain time; scientists usually use a period of 30 years when establishing a region's climate.

🌐 Tree transpiration

In a single hour on a very warm day, the leaves of one large oak tree can release as much as 53 gallons (200 l) of water as water vapor through the process of transpiration. One acre (0.4 ha) of tropical forest can release 21,000 gallons (80,000 l) of water vapor into the atmosphere in a day.

▼ During the water cycle, heat makes water evaporate into the atmosphere. It then falls back to Earth as precipitation, where it returns to lakes, rivers, and seas, or is collected from the soil by plants. Once this has happened, the cycle begins again.

What is the water cycle?

The water on our planet is always on the move. It circulates constantly through different states and in different locations. This is known as the water cycle.

The water cycle is driven by energy from the sun. Heat from the sun causes water to turn from a liquid into gaseous water vapor. This gradual transformation—which occurs without the water boiling—is called evaporation. Around four-fifths of all evaporation comes from the oceans; the remaining one-fifth comes from inland water bodies such as rivers and lakes, and from vegetation. The evaporation of water into the atmosphere from the leaves and stems of plants is called transpiration. Plants absorb water from the soil through their roots and transport it through their stems and trunks to their leaves.

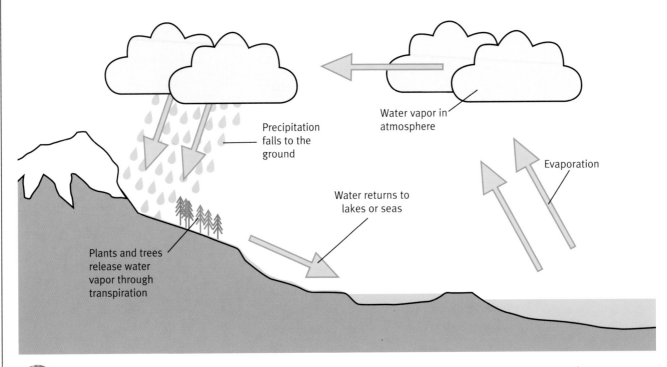

Water vapor in atmosphere

Precipitation falls to the ground

Water returns to lakes or seas

Evaporation

Plants and trees release water vapor through transpiration

◀ Rainfall—seen here at the bottom center—
is the result of the cooling and condensation of
moisture by wind.

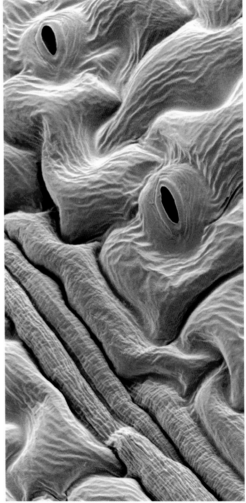

Most water is transpired by plants through small pores or
openings called stomata, found on the underside of leaves.

Winds transport the evaporated water around the globe,
influencing the levels of humidity (the amount of moisture
carried in the atmosphere) throughout the world. Clouds
form when warm air containing water vapor rises and then
cools. The vapor condenses to form millions of tiny water
droplets; these collide with each other to create larger
droplets. Eventually, they become too heavy for the air
to support and fall back to Earth as rain.

Water that falls onto Earth's surface from clouds is called
precipitation. The type of precipitation that occurs
depends largely on temperature and air pressure. Rain
is the most common form, but snow, sleet, and hail are
also forms of precipitation. Snowflakes form when water
droplets in clouds freeze into ice crystals and then fall to

▲ This microscopic image shows the tiny pores,
or stomata, on the underside of leaves, magnified
to about 400 times their actual size. These act like
the pores in human skin, allowing water to pass
out of the leaf in a process called transpiration.

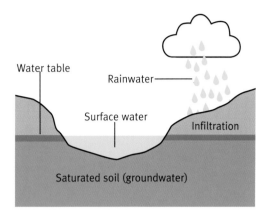

When rainwater hits the ground, some of it will penetrate the surface (infiltration). A certain amount (groundwater) is drawn back up through the roots of trees and plants. The rest sinks to the water table.

This is the "Middle of the World" monument, situated on the equator in Ecuador. Here, and all along the equator, temperatures are high because the sun's rays strike Earth almost directly.

the ground through cold air. Sleet is a mixture of snow and rain. It is created when rain encounters a layer of very cold air close to the ground, which causes some, but not all, of the rain to freeze.

Once the water reaches the ground, one of a number of processes may occur. Some of the water may be trapped or intercepted by plants and then transpired back into the atmosphere. Some water also forms small pools or puddles on the ground; much of this evaporates back into the atmosphere. Water may penetrate the surface of the land in a process called infiltration. Infiltration can occur at different rates depending on the composition of the soil. For example, sandy soil with lots of air spaces between the sand grains allows rapid infiltration, whereas in clay soil, with much smaller spaces between the particles, infiltration is much slower. A portion of this water, called groundwater, will be drawn up by the roots of plants and released back into the atmosphere via transpiration. Some groundwater sinks until it reaches the water table—the top surface of the saturation zone, where all the air spaces in the soil and rock have become filled with water. Much groundwater travels sideways along locations known as aquifers and eventually seeps into oceans, rivers, and streams. The rest of the water that remains on Earth's surface is called runoff. Runoff eventually empties into streams, rivers, and lakes, which gradually carry it back toward the oceans.

What factors influence climate?

Climates vary around the world, and many factors influence them. Among these are the region's latitude (its distance from the equator), the circulation of air currents and winds, and the movement of water in the world's oceans.

How the sun's rays strike Earth's surface can determine the temperature of a region, which affects its climate and weather patterns. Because the surface of Earth is curved, different parts of the planet receive different amounts of the sun's rays. Around the center of Earth—the equator—temperatures remain high and fairly consistent, because the sun's rays strike this region almost directly year-round, and the sun's energy is more concentrated. Farther away from

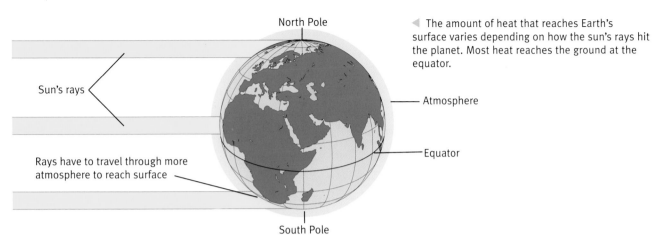

North Pole

Sun's rays

Rays have to travel through more atmosphere to reach surface

Atmosphere

Equator

South Pole

◀ The amount of heat that reaches Earth's surface varies depending on how the sun's rays hit the planet. Most heat reaches the ground at the equator.

the equator, the angle at which the sun's rays strike Earth's surface is greater. This means that they travel through more of Earth's heat-absorbing atmosphere and that their energy is spread over a wider surface area, which reduces the warming effect of the rays. This is similar to a flashlight beam that appears elongated and dim when the flashlight is held at an oblique angle to a surface. The polar regions—the farthest points from the equator—are the coldest on Earth.

▼ Earth is coldest at the poles, in areas like Antarctica, because the sun's rays pass through more atmosphere in the polar regions, which absorbs more heat.

▲ This is a low-pressure weather system over Australia. The swirling clouds bring stormy but humid weather. Sometimes the storms become so intense that they form a hurricane or typhoon.

🌐 North Sea storm surge

Storm surges are abnormal rises in sea levels. They occur most frequently in areas of the world that are prone to massive storms including hurricanes, such as Asia and the Gulf of Mexico. However, these are not the only places that can suffer. In January 1953, a giant storm surge in the southern North Sea resulted in a sea level rise of more than 10 feet (3 m). Catastrophic flooding occurred on the coasts of England and the Netherlands, claiming more than 2,200 lives.

What are high and low air pressure?

Air pressure is the weight or mass of the atmosphere pushing down on Earth's surface. Because air in Earth's atmosphere is always on the move, air pressure constantly varies from place to place. At the surface, air moves from areas of high pressure (called anticyclones) to areas of low pressure (called cyclones or depressions). This movement of air is wind.

Scientists have identified a number of circulation cells in the atmosphere, where air moves across the latitudes. As air rises and falls within these cells, it affects the air pressure at the ground surface. In areas where air rises (for example, at the equator) low pressure areas are formed. Where air sinks (for example, at about 30° north and south), areas of high pressure are formed.

Areas of high pressure tend to bring hot, dry weather in summer and cold, dry weather in winter. This is because air is usually sinking and is therefore unlikely to form clouds and rain. Low pressure areas, with their associated rising air, tend to bring clouds, rain, or snow. Over seas and oceans, intense low pressure areas can result in storm surges that may lead to rises in sea level; this is a major cause of coastal flooding (see page 22).

How do ocean currents affect climate?

Earth's climate is affected by the water in the oceans and its ability to absorb large quantities of the sun's heat. Amazingly, the top six feet (2 m) of an ocean store more heat than all of Earth's atmosphere! Ocean currents carry much of this heat around the world and toward the polar regions. In this way, heat is redistributed, and the global heat balance is maintained. This heat warms land masses as well as the lower atmosphere above the ocean. One major ocean current, the Gulf Stream, carries warmth toward northern Europe, giving the region a mild climate. Oceans tend to moderate the climate of coastal regions, reducing the extremes of temperature found there. Areas far inland usually experience more extreme temperature differences between their winters and summers and are usually drier. Occasionally, major ocean currents alter their direction, which can have a significant effect on the climate.

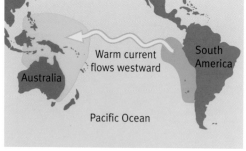

In 1998, heavy spring rains caused by El Niño resulted in a series of flash floods in California.

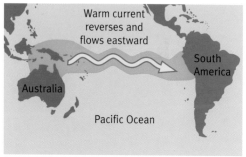

In the Pacific, surface ocean currents normally transport warmer water west toward Australia. El Niño is the name given to a complex series of changes in weather conditions caused by the reversal in the currents of the Pacific Ocean. During El Niño, the warm current flows eastward, creating more water vapor in the air over parts of South America, Central America, and the United States. This leads to heavier rainfalls and floods in these regions, while drought conditions occur in the west Pacific, including Australia and Indonesia. Climate can be affected all over the world by the El Niño phenomenon. The giant El Niño of 1997–98 disrupted weather patterns around the globe, resulting in droughts, floods, and

Ocean currents affect the climates of different regions. When major currents change, it can have a huge impact on climate. In the Pacific Ocean, the reversal of currents is called El Niño. During this time, the warm current flows eastward, resulting in floods in America and reduced rainfall in Southeast Asia and Australia.

13

🌀 Water proportions

Seas and oceans contain 97.5 percent of Earth's water; the land holds 2.4 percent; and the atmosphere contains less than a thousandth of a percent.

▲ Deforestation is believed to be a major cause of the greenhouse effect. As trees are cut down, more greenhouse gases can be trapped in the atmosphere, warming the planet.

storms that killed an estimated 2,100 people.

How is global warming related to floods and droughts?

Temperature records indicate that the planet is getting warmer; scientists call this trend "global warming." In the past 100 years, there have also been more reported instances of droughts and floods than ever before. Many scientists believe that the two phenomena are linked and that part of the change in global climate is due to the greenhouse effect.

Global warming is a complex process, and no one is certain what will occur in the future. Some scientists think that global warming could enhance the speed at which the water cycle occurs. Rates of evaporation could increase, resulting in widespread drought conditions as well as

▶ In 2002, Australia experienced its worst drought since reliable records began in 1910. Australian scientists believe that global warming was a major cause of the drought. It was concentrated in eastern Australia, in the Murray-Darling Basin—the nation's agricultural heartland, which produces two-fifths of Australia's agricultural output.

potentially making weather more unpredictable. Warmer and wetter conditions caused by global warming may increase flooding in some areas, while an increase in global temperatures will cause sea levels to rise (water expands as it warms up). The Intergovernmental Panel on Climate Change reports that sea levels could rise by more than 24 inches (60 cm) by the 22nd century. This would result in huge areas of land being submerged—the U.S. Environmental Protection Agency estimates that as much as 22,000 square miles (57,000 sq km) of America's eastern coastline could be threatened. This is just a tiny fraction of the land that could be submerged around the world, which would particularly affect the millions of people living in low-lying delta regions such as Bangladesh.

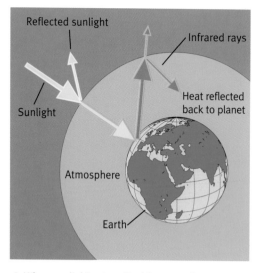

▲ When sunlight enters Earth's atmosphere and strikes the planet's surface, some of the sun's energy is reflected back as heat in the form of infrared radiation. Greenhouse gases absorb this radiation, trapping heat in the atmosphere and warming the planet.

🌐 Greenhouse gases

Greenhouse gases, such as carbon dioxide, methane, and nitrous oxide, are naturally present in Earth's atmosphere and perform a vital role by helping to trap some of the sun's energy as heat, effectively warming the planet's surface. Due to an increase in the concentrations of greenhouse gases in the atmosphere, more heat is being trapped. This has risen by as much as 25 percent in the past 150 years. Deforestation (the removal of trees and plant cover from the land) and the burning of large quantities of fossil fuels in industry and by motor vehicles are major causes of this increase. Scientists are concerned about the rate of increase and the way it might affect our planet in the future.

▶ Air pollution from the burning of fossil fuels in industry and by motor vehicles is one of the major causes of the greenhouse effect.

15

Floods: Causes and Impacts

After fire, floods are the most common and widespread of all natural disasters. In the U.S. alone, property damage from flooding totals more than $5 billion per year.

Rivers change as they progress from young, fast-moving bodies of water in steeper areas to slow-moving, mature rivers, which often meander in large curves across flat lands before reaching the sea. Material eroded by rivers in the uplands builds up as sediment, which is then carried by the river in its lower course. Large rivers transport enormous amounts of sediment—the Mississippi River, for example, empties approximately 10.6 billion cubic feet (300 million cu m) of sediment into the Gulf of Mexico every year. This sediment is finally deposited in one of two ways. It can be left at the mouth of the river, where it empties into the sea;

▼ In China, huge areas of a floodplain are often terraced and used to cultivate crops such as rice, which grows well in saturated soil. This is one example of how flooding can have positive effects.

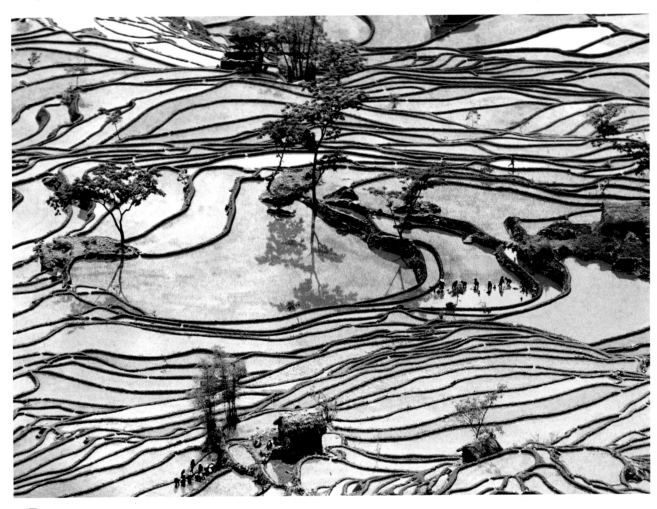

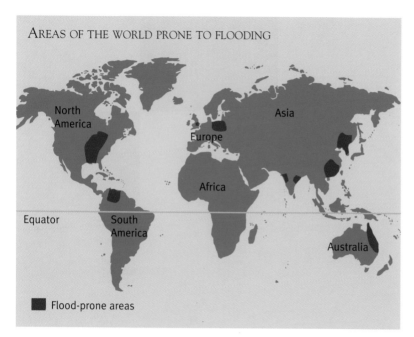

AREAS OF THE WORLD PRONE TO FLOODING

North America

Asia

Europe

Africa

Equator

South America

Australia

■ Flood-prone areas

This map shows the parts of the world that are particularly prone to flooding disasters. Such floods are usually caused by sudden, heavy, or prolonged rainfall.

over time, layers of sediment can build up to form an area of flat land called a delta. Sediment can also be deposited when the river bursts its banks or floods along its course. During a river flood, the sediment is deposited on the land on either side of the river.

Over many years of repeated floods, layers of extremely fertile land build up; these are known as floodplains or alluvial plains. Floodplains have been vital to the development of human life. Many early civilizations grew up around them, close to rivers such as the Nile in Egypt, the Indus and the Ganges in India, and China's Huang He. Today, these and other floodplains are inhabited by millions of people who rely on the fertile land for food, even though the risk of flooding remains a constant concern.

What are cyclical floods?

Many floods are cyclical, which means they occur regularly, often caused by a cycle of rains or melting snow and ice. For example, monsoons that occur in Asia bring regular and welcome rains essential to regional crop growing. However, they can also cause flooding of river deltas and floodplains. For thousands of years, the Nile River's annual flooding not only brought vital waters but also rich, fertile sediments to the fields on either side of the river. The Egyptians referred to the annual flooding as the "Gift of the Nile" (see page 38).

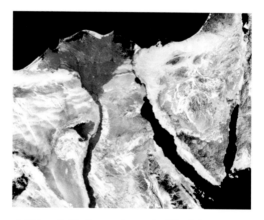

This satellite image shows the Nile delta. The fertile region, where the Nile River floods its banks, can be seen in red at the top left. Settlements grew up around areas like this because the land was fertile and good for farming. The Egyptian capital of Cairo is the tiny gray area right at the base of the delta.

One way of measuring the magnitude, or scale, of a flood is to compare it to how often a similar-sized flood is expected to occur. Floods can occur every 10, 100, 500, or 1,000 years. For example, a 10-year flood is a level of river discharge that has a probability of occurring once every 10 years on average. Such an event is much smaller than a 100-year flood, which is only likely to occur on average once every 100 years. Remember, however, that these probabilities are long-term, and there is no reason why two large floods couldn't happen in consecutive years. The Big Thompson River valley flood (see page 20) was a once every 1,000-year flood.

▼ There are several reasons why regions around rivers can flood. These include heavy rains, melting ice and snow, storm surges, human land use, and the failure of dams.

What are the main causes of river floods?

River floods can be caused by a number of different factors. The most common of these is a torrential storm or a long period of heavy rain. Flooding occurs when there is too much water for a river channel to contain, and excess water spills over the top of the banks. During a storm, large amounts of water fall on a drainage basin in a very short period of time, and the river channels cannot cope with the volume of water surging down the streams and tributaries.

The rate at which soil absorbs water decreases with continuous wetting. The longer a rainstorm lasts, the more likely it is that rainwater will flow across the ground as surface runoff and enter streams and rivers. The amount of water that can be held in the soil depends on its porosity—the proportion of pore spaces in the soil. The ability of water to flow through the soil depends on its permeability; if there are lots of pores or underground channels, then water will pass through the soil freely. Under such conditions, the soil is said to be permeable; if water does not pass through the soil, it is said to be impermeable. When the entire underground area is saturated, more water is forced to remain on the surface.

Different land surfaces hold different amounts of water and absorb it at different rates. Flooding is common in winter and early spring when the ground can be frozen and impermeable. This means that most rainwater and meltwater from snow and ice become surface runoff.

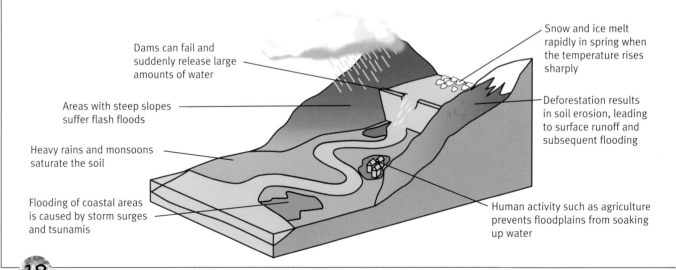

Dams can fail and suddenly release large amounts of water

Areas with steep slopes suffer flash floods

Heavy rains and monsoons saturate the soil

Flooding of coastal areas is caused by storm surges and tsunamis

Snow and ice melt rapidly in spring when the temperature rises sharply

Deforestation results in soil erosion, leading to surface runoff and subsequent flooding

Human activity such as agriculture prevents floodplains from soaking up water

🌐 China's river floods

In the last 2,000 years, the Yangtze River in China has flooded more than 1,000 times. However, another river, the Huang He, has been responsible for China's most disastrous floods. The river has a very high silt content, which chokes the channel, causing the river to overflow. In 1887, flooding killed nearly two million people; in 1931, the death toll was almost four million; and in 1938, it was almost one million.

▶ In China, a boy sits on the roof of his house—the only place to escape the floodwaters.

How can snowmelt and ice jams cause flooding?

Rapidly melting snow or thawing ice can create enormous amounts of water. This can upset the balance of the water cycle in a region and may result in flooding. An ice jam can occur when parts of a frozen river thaw and melt at different rates than other parts. High levels of water become trapped behind still-frozen river ice and can flood the surrounding area. In February 2003, an ice jam on the Exploits River in Canada caused a major flood that swept through the town of Badger in Newfoundland; 1,200 people were evacuated from their homes.

▼ This is a melting polar ice cap. When large bodies of frozen water like this begin to melt, they can sweep through a region and overflow river banks, creating massive floods.

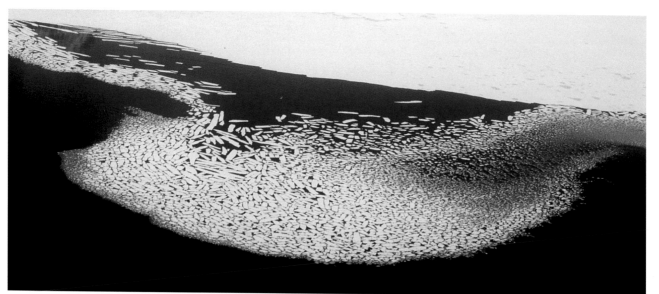

What are flash floods?

Flash floods are floods that occur quickly, usually within six hours of the start of heavy rainfall. A cloudburst flood is a type of flash flood caused by very intense rainfall, usually more than 10 inches (25 cm) per hour. A relatively small number of flash floods are caused by sudden snowmelt or ice jams.

▶ Flash floods, like this one in Montana, are caused by sudden, heavy downpours of rain.

Flash floods are more common in mountainous areas, where steep slopes cause water to travel at high speeds. Although flash floods tend to occur quickly and last only a short time, they can still be devastating because they usually come with little warning. If a man-made dam holding back huge quantities of water fails, it can also cause destructive flash floods.

Can human activity cause floods?

Human impact on land areas can create conditions in which floods are more likely. For example, the removal of tree cover through deforestation (see page 33) deprives land of the vegetation that intercepts and soaks up large amounts of rainfall. Without trees, more water than the land can absorb through infiltration may reach the ground during heavy rains. The excess water becomes surface runoff, carrying loose soil that is no longer bound together by tree and plant roots. This soil can clog rivers and lakes with sediment, making floods more likely.

🌀 The Big Thompson flash flood

The Big Thompson River valley was a popular destination for campers and walkers in Colorado. In July 1976, a thunderstorm resulted in 12 inches (30 cm) of rainfall in less than 5 hours. Two-thirds of that rain fell in less than an hour. A severe flash flood raged down the river valley, sweeping 10-foot-wide (3 m) boulders in front of it. Houses, vehicles, and campers had no chance to escape. During that short time, more than 140 people were killed, 418 houses were destroyed, and more than $40 million in damage was wrought.

Some floods are a result of deliberate or accidental human action. Occasionally, they are caused by the construction of dams to form a reservoir intended to supply settlements or industry with water, or to concentrate the natural fall of a river at one location to maximize the amount of energy that can be used by a hydroelectric power plant. Poor dam and reservoir construction can cause floods that lead to widespread destruction. In 1963, in northeastern Italy, a giant landslide fell into a water reservoir held in place by the Vaiont Dam. The landslide generated a wave that powered over the top of the dam and destroyed a number of nearby settlements, killing more than 2,500 people. Amazingly, the dam remained intact. The area had been prone to landslides in the past and was a high-risk site for building a large dam and reservoir.

Urbanization—the growth of towns and cities—has resulted in much previously undeveloped land being covered in stone, concrete, and other impermeable materials to form parking lots, roads, and sidewalks. Unless drainage systems are carefully planned and constructed, rainwater cannot be absorbed into the ground fast enough and becomes surface runoff. Heavy and prolonged rainfall can easily cause an urban flood, which fills parking lots and overflows to submerge nearby roads and flood buildings below ground level.

▲ Flooding can cause serious damage to property in built-up areas, where concrete roads prevent water from being easily absorbed. This flood warning sign is in a residential area in Britain.

🛟 The Buffalo Creek disaster

A dam at Buffalo Creek in West Virginia was used to store waste material from coal mining, which included a large amount of water. In February 1972, after three days of heavy rains, the dam collapsed, sending tons of water down the valley. The resulting flood killed 118 people in nearby towns and caused nearly $70 million in damage.

▶ A row of houses in the coal mining town of Buffalo Creek, West Virginia, is destroyed when the dam collapses, sending a cascade of water downstream.

What causes coastal flooding?

Seas and oceans cover almost three-quarters of Earth's surface, and nearly half of the world's population lives within 37 miles (60 km) of a coastline. When the sea level rises and overflows into coastal regions, floods can cause widespread destruction and loss of life. Such rises in sea level and coastal flooding are caused by several phenomena, including global warming (see page 14), tsunamis (see page 24), and hurricanes (see page 23).

Ocean storms can transport large quantities of water to coastal regions. Such storms are usually caused by an intense area of low pressure, which can raise the sea level in that region. These storm-related rises in sea level are called storm surges, and they can result in coastal flooding in many parts of the world.

▲ The city of Venice, Italy, has been subject to coastal flooding caused by rises in sea level and the fact that the city itself is gradually sinking. In 2003, construction began on a sea gate, which it is hoped will protect this ancient city and its beautiful historic buildings from the threat of further floods.

▶ Hundreds of people flee their homes as floods hit Chibuto, Mozambique. These floods were caused by unexpected levels of rainfall, which made the sea level rise and move inland.

🌀 Sea level rise in Bangladesh

A storm at the mouth of the River Ganges in Bangladesh in August 2004 caused a flood that eventually covered almost two-thirds of the country. The disaster affected nearly 30 million people, many of whom found that their homes were destroyed and that they were cut off from food and other supplies. The problems in Bangladesh continued for months, as diseases carried in the water infected the population.

▼ Parts of Bangladesh have suffered from periodic flooding in the delta region. Here, people are forced to travel by boat on floodwaters in August 2004.

🌀 Hurricanes

Hurricanes, also known as tropical cyclones or typhoons, are fierce, spiraling storms that form over the oceans of the tropics. Hurricanes have an intense low pressure core, sucking in warm, moist air that rises rapidly to form towering thunderstorm clouds. Hurricanes are associated with high wind speeds, averaging 75 miles (120 km) per hour, with gusts in excess of 125 miles (200 km) per hour. Torrential rainfall occurs, often leading to flooding as rivers burst their banks.

◀ The high winds of Hurricane Frances cause flooding in a parking lot in Florida in September 2004.

Can tides cause floods?

Tides are the regular rise and fall of the sea level caused by the gravitational pull of the sun and the moon on Earth's oceans. Tides move inland and back twice every 24 hours. In the open sea, the movement of the water is hardly noticeable. However, in some coastal areas—such as those with narrow bays—the tidal difference is significant. The tidal range is the vertical height difference between high tide—when the sea level is highest—and low tide, when it is at its lowest. Tidal ranges can be as little as 20 inches (50 cm), but along some coastlines, they can be far greater. The tidal range on the south coast of Britain near the outlet of the River Thames is approximately 20 feet (6 m). In the Bay of Fundy in southeastern Canada, the tidal range is more than 52 feet (16 m). Regular high tides are predictable and rarely produce flooding on their own. However, when a very high tide coincides with a moderate or severe storm, flooding can occur.

▶ During high tide, seawaters move up the beaches, drawing closer to towns and cities; at low tide, they recede. This picture shows high tide near a village in the Pribilof Islands in Alaska.

▶ Every 14 days, the moon and the sun are aligned, and both exert a gravitational pull on Earth's seas and oceans. As a result, higher-than-usual tides—called spring tides—occur, which can cause flooding.

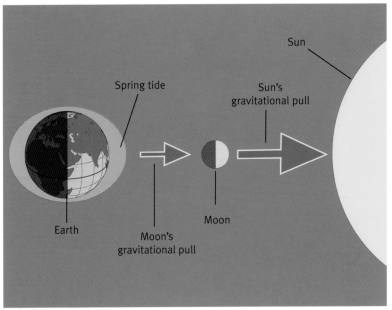

Spring tide

Sun's gravitational pull

Sun

Earth

Moon's gravitational pull

Moon

What are tsunamis?

Tsunamis are destructive waves that sweep in from the ocean. They are sometimes known as tidal waves, although this is misleading, since they are not caused by or related to tidal movement. They are usually the result of a volcanic eruption, a giant landslide, or an earthquake that occurs under the sea.

The Asian tsunami

On December 26, 2004, an earthquake measuring 9.0 on the Richter scale occurred in the Indian Ocean near Sumatra. It caused a series of tsunamis that devastated 11 countries across Asia. The effects were felt as far away as Africa, nearly 3,100 miles (5,000 km) from the epicenter. Since no warning system exists in the Indian Ocean, the damage was severe. An estimated 220,000 people were killed immediately. Experts predict that a further 150,000 people will die from disease caused by lack of clean water, food, or shelter.

A tsunami can travel tens or even hundreds of miles across the ocean, reaching speeds of up to 500 miles (800 km) per hour. As a tsunami leaves the deep water of the open ocean and travels into the shallower water near the coast, it transforms. Its speed decreases, although it still travels rapidly and with great force, but as it slows down, its height increases. Out at sea, a tsunami may appear as a wave only one to three feet (0.5–1 m) high and be hardly noticeable. However, by the time it reaches the coast, it might have grown to a wall of water more than 50 feet (15 m) high.

Tsunamis lose energy as they hit the shoreline, but they still arrive with vast amounts of energy, capable of destroying entire coastal towns and traveling inland several miles. Tsunamis can have great powers of erosion, stripping land of its vegetation and beaches of their sand.

The most recent major tsunami occurred in December 2004. Caused by an undersea earthquake off the Indonesian coast, the tsunami surged across the Indian Ocean at great speeds. The province of Aceh in northern Indonesia was the closest inhabited area to the earthquake's epicenter and was the first hit. Within the next few hours, the tsunami devastated coastlines all across Asia, with waves reaching heights of 50 feet (15 m) as they swept inland. Buildings were destroyed in an instant, and whole communities were wiped out.

▲ A massive wave strikes Penang in Malaysia in December 2004. There was little warning that the tsunamis were about to hit, and many people did not understand the danger they were in. People were killed or injured as the waves crashed over buildings, or they were sucked out to sea as the water receded.

▼ Men in Nicaragua try to salvage parts of their home after it was destroyed by a tsunami in 1992.

Droughts: Causes and Impacts

Many parts of the world experience a dry climate with a lack of rainfall. Desert regions—areas that receive less than 10 inches (25 cm) of rainfall per year—cover more than a tenth of the land on Earth. Many species of animals and plants have learned to adapt to the harsh desert climates and environments. However, during a drought, much harsher conditions prevail, and many people may die or be forced to move away from their homes.

▲ A drought is defined as a period in which an area experiences lower levels of rainfall than normal, causing the ground to dry out. Here, a farmer stands beside what remains of a lake in North Dakota during a period of drought in the 1990s.

Drought can best be defined as an extended period in which rainfall levels are below those normally expected in a particular region. This can lead to a long-term depletion of groundwater and the stunting or dying of plants due to lack of water. Although we tend to associate droughts with the desert areas of the world, they can occur almost anywhere. In England, for example, where rainfall is usually quite high, a drought struck in 1976; reservoirs dried up and people had to collect freshwater from vertical pipes in the street or from water tankers.

Droughts can be classified regionally according to the amount of rainfall a region normally receives. For example, in the U.S., a drought is defined as 21 days with only 30 percent of the average rainfall for that area. In India, a drought occurs when monsoon rains are much weaker than usual. When rainfall is more than 30 percent lower than

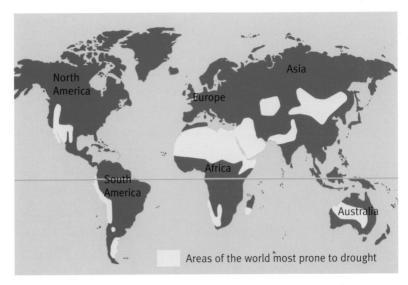

Areas of the world most prone to drought

▶ This map shows the parts of the world that are most prone to drought, including the vast areas of desert in places such as North Africa and central Australia.

normal and more than 20 percent of an area of the country is under drought, the situation is called an all-India drought. The beginning of a drought is especially difficult to determine. Weeks or many months may elapse before it is clear that a drought is occurring. A period of lower than average rainfall may not always signal the start of a drought, as dry spells occur throughout the world.

▲ The Atacama Desert in northern Chile is one of the driest regions on Earth. In 1971, rain fell for the first time in nearly 400 years.

Where do droughts occur?

During the mid-1980s, people in wealthier, more developed countries such as the U.S. and many European nations were shocked by television and newspaper images from Ethiopia. These showed massive suffering and death from famine (a severe shortage of food), disease, and lack of water. This was caused in part by a civil war in the country, which meant that food distribution was not efficient, but the key factor in the famine was a fierce drought that had struck the country. As a result of this high-profile example, many people associate droughts with parts of Africa, particularly the fringes of the world's largest desert, the Sahara. The reality is that they are far more

🌐 Measuring drought

The Palmer Drought Severity Index is one of several measuring systems for droughts. It uses temperature and rainfall data to indicate which areas of a country are more likely to be affected by drought. The index uses 0 as normal; drought is shown in terms of negative numbers. For example, -2 is a moderate drought, -3 is a severe drought, and -4 is an extreme drought.

27

▶ In many drought-ridden regions, facilities such as this water pump in Kabul can save lives, although many people have to travel long distances to collect water for drinking and washing.

common and widespread than this. For example, in 2002, severe droughts again struck Ethiopia, but also affected parts of the U.S., Australia, Central America, and Asia.

Despite this, droughts do occur most frequently in regions on the edges of hot deserts, usually the driest parts of the planet. Rain falling from clouds above these areas often has to pass through thousands of feet of air. Because of the heat and the distance it falls, much of the rain evaporates before it reaches the ground.

▼ The Sahara is the largest desert in the world. Around its edges, where people live, droughts are common because much of the rain in the atmosphere evaporates before it reaches the ground.

During the water cycle, water is released as vapor back into the atmosphere by means of evaporation and through transpiration from plants. The total amount

of water returned to the atmosphere by these processes is called evapotranspiration. The rate of evapotranspiration can vary greatly depending on the temperature, humidity, and winds in an area. When evapotranspiration rates are high—increased by sunlight and long periods of heat—soil loses moisture rapidly, and extremely dry conditions develop. As plants die, food supplies for people and animals disappear.

Drought in North America

North America experienced a three-year drought between 1987 and 1989. The drought began along the west coast of the U.S. and spread into northwestern regions and southern Canada. At its peak, an estimated 36 percent of the U.S. was in drought. Wildfires raged through the world-famous Yellowstone Park in 1988, but the greatest damage was to agriculture. The total cost of the drought was estimated at more than $36 billion.

◀ These corn plants have withered and died due to lack of rainfall in Texas. At its worst, the drought in North America covered more than a third of the country.

What causes droughts?

Droughts involve a complex series of processes that are still being researched. Climate change brought on by global warming may be increasing the risk of droughts in some regions. Variations in climate and weather caused by changes in winds and ocean currents such as El Niño (see page 13) are believed to be the cause of many droughts across the world.

Another weather condition that can give rise to droughts is an area of high air pressure called a blocking high. A blocking high usually remains stationary for a long period of time and effectively forces any areas of low pressure, which carry clouds and rain, around it. An area of land that lies underneath a particularly strong and long-term blocking high may experience a drought. This

▲ Droughts are often caused by a lack of precipitation, but they can also be a result of hot, dry winds, which remove moisture from the soil so nothing can grow.

▼ This diagram shows how air rises and falls over mountains, creating rain shadow areas. Most of the rain falls in the mountains; any precipitation that remains is picked up by the warm, dry air, leaving a desert area.

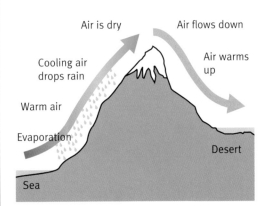

Air is dry   Air flows down

Cooling air drops rain   Air warms up

Warm air

Evaporation

Desert

Sea

phenomenon is believed to be responsible for most of the droughts that affect California, for example. A blocking high created drought conditions in Britain and much of western Europe in 1976 (see page 26).

Some areas of the world are prone to droughts because of their geographical location. A rain shadow area, for example, can occur when a range of mountains lies in the path of rain-carrying winds from the sea. The air is forced to cool down as it rises over the mountains, and it releases almost all of the water it is carrying as rain. When the air starts to sink on the leeward side of the mountains, it becomes warmer and drier. This is called the rain shadow effect, and it explains why areas on the leeward side of mountains are much drier than those on the windward side. A rain shadow area may become a desert or may experience droughts. The Great Dividing Range in Australia and the Rocky Mountains of North America both create rain shadow areas that suffer from periodic drought conditions.

Clouds containing water vapor can be carried long distances. However, the farther they travel inland and away from the oceans, the more likely they are to have released some or most of their moisture as precipitation. In regions lying thousands of miles from the coast, there may be very little rainfall. These places are sometimes referred to as "continental drought regions." The Gobi Desert in Mongolia falls into this category.

◀ In 2001, the extreme heat in and around desert regions in Australia caused bush fires, which spread dangerously close to urban areas. Some scientists attribute the increase in the number of this type of fire to global warming.

🌐 Famine

A famine is a long period of time in which an area suffers from a lack of food. Many factors can contribute to famine, including war, the general poverty in a region, earthquakes, and other natural disasters. However, drought is often a major cause of famine. Almost 70 percent of all water used by humans is diverted for agriculture. Without adequate water supplies, crops fail, livestock dies, and food supplies are drastically reduced. This is why famines frequently follow prolonged droughts.

Drought in eastern Africa

In 1984, a severe drought hit eastern Africa, particularly the nations of Ethiopia, Sudan, and Somalia. In northern Ethiopia, for example, there was an almost total failure of crops, as plants did not receive the levels of water they required for growth. Hundreds of thousands of people were forced to leave their homelands, and more than six million became reliant on refugee camps and food aid from feeding centers supplied by countries such as England and the U.S. The death toll in the region had risen to almost one million by the end of the drought.

Workers carry sacks of wheat to famine-stricken villages in Ethiopia during the drought.

What happens after a drought?

Many regions of the world mostly or fully recover after a drought. Drought-stricken areas in wealthier countries receive aid with which they can replenish lands, as well as build water systems that may make a future drought less damaging. In poorer nations, the prospects can be bleak. What funding there might be is often spent on disaster relief—providing some form of food, shelter, and medical attention to keep people alive—without any longer-term planning. Furthermore, money is often spent on large, glamorous projects that benefit wealthy city dwellers without helping the majority of the rural poor.

Heavy rainfall may signify the end of a drought, but it is rarely the end of the problems. When rain hits sun-baked ground, the water is often unable to infiltrate the soil. It remains on the surface and can lead to soil erosion and powerful floods, causing more devastation. In 2003, after lengthy droughts in Kenya and Ethiopia, both regions were subject to heavy rains, resulting in floods. About 60,000 people in Kenya and 95,000 in Ethiopia were rendered homeless.

A man and a child sit on the ground in Thailand; the land has been baked by the sun and cracked due to lack of rain, so that it can no longer support life.

What is desertification?

Desertification is the expansion of desert-like conditions into areas that had previously been able to support life. While desertification can be a natural consequence of climate change, it is often brought about inadvertently by human activities, including the overgrazing of livestock, deforestation (the removal of trees and plant cover), and surface land mining.

Along with drought, these activities may result in large areas losing vegetation. The roots of trees and other plants bind soil together, enabling water to be absorbed and further plant life to grow. As land is cleared of its vegetation, the topsoil becomes exposed to the elements and can be washed or blown away, clogging rivers and other bodies of water with sediment. When topsoil is removed, water cannot be retained in the remaining soil, and fertile land becomes arid and desert-like.

▲ In Morocco, villagers have built barriers to try to prevent desertification. The United Nations estimates that desertification claims as much as 23,000 square miles (60,000 sq km) of land every year.

▲ In a 2003 study, scientists in Australia and Canada stated that pollution from Western countries may have caused the droughts that ravaged Africa's Sahel region in the 1970s and 1980s. Research suggests that sulfur dioxide from factories in Europe and the U.S. has cooled parts of the Northern Hemisphere, driving the tropical rain belt southward away from the Sahel.

🌐 Drought and desertification in the Sahel

The Sahel is a broad band of dry land that stretches across Africa south of the Sahara Desert. Rainfall is low, usually less than 20 inches (50 cm) a year, and records show that it has declined 20 to 50 percent since the early 20th century. The rainfall is also unpredictable, with variations from year to year of 50 percent or more. Evaporation rates are extremely high, and severe droughts that claimed the lives of thousands of people occurred in 1972, 1975, 1984, and 1985. These devastating dry periods, as well as a significant increase in the number of people and grazing animals in the area, have allowed desertification to take hold of areas of the Sahel. In effect, the Sahara Desert is advancing southward in some places at a rate of about three miles (5 km) a year.

Living with Floods and Droughts

Millions of people live in regions affected by droughts and floods. In fact, humans have shown a remarkable ability to adapt to life in these areas. For centuries, nomadic peoples in desert and drought-threatened locations have migrated over large areas, developing techniques that have enabled them to survive even in the harshest conditions. In parts of Southeast Asia prone to regular flooding, houses are built on stilts, keeping them away from typical high water levels.

How can the impact of drought be reduced?

Lower than average or nonexistent rainfall can strike many regions, but measures can be taken to reduce its impact. Managing the soil by keeping it in place and in good condition is vital. Steps to prevent overgrazing and overuse of the soil are required in some regions, but in poorer countries, which contain thousands of farmers, it is extremely difficult to prevent people from overusing the land to survive. .

▼ Reforestation projects, such as this one in Costa Rica, are being carried out in many regions to reverse the effects of deforestation.

In many locations around the world, reforestation projects are being introduced. These involve planting new trees to grow forests and increase vegetation in areas where deforestation has occurred. Windbreaks can also help reduce the amount of soil blown away by winds, limiting the impact of soil erosion. Mulching—the placing of organic matter, such as leaves, straw, and sawdust, over the ground—is a practice that can enrich the soil, keep it in place, and reduce water loss from evaporation.

The careful selection of crops suitable for the soil and climate conditions is also crucial. Dry farming depends upon efficient storage of the limited moisture in the soil, and the choice of crops and growing methods that make the best use of this moisture is important. Drought-resistant crops, such as sorghum, can reduce transpiration. Such crops may nearly cease growing during periods when there is little moisture available, but instead of dying, as many crops would do, they start to grow again when conditions become favorable.

▲ This abandoned farmhouse in Texas, photographed in 1938, shows the effect of the Dust Bowl on American farmland—plants and crops withered and died as the topsoil was blown away. The land could no longer support farming, and people were forced to leave their homes.

🌐 Dust Bowl America

A severe drought combined with poor soil-conservation techniques can lead to extreme soil erosion, which can have devastating effects on the land. This is what happened in the Great Plains region of the U.S. during the 1930s. Intensive farming of grain crops and overgrazing by cattle left the soil in such poor condition that when a lengthy drought occurred, winds blew away as much as four inches (10 cm) of the topsoil. This resulted in a "Dust Bowl." In May 1934, a cloud of topsoil from the Great Plains blanketed the eastern regions of the U.S. as far as 1,500 miles (2,400 km) away. Thousands of farming families had to leave their land. It took many years of soil conservation measures and huge amounts of government funding to restore the land to a level that was suitable for farming once again.

Is there enough water to go around?

There is enough freshwater globally to supply the current world population; the problem lies in its distribution. In parts of Africa, the Middle East, and Asia, the lack of access to clean water is a huge problem, affecting more than one billion people.

Sanitation and good sewage systems are necessary to remove waste and prevent many harmful diseases. But these systems cost money to build and use large amounts of water themselves. According to the World Health Organization (WHO), more than 2.4 billion people do not have access to safe sanitation systems. As a result, as many as three million people every year die from water-related diseases such as cholera. As the world population increases, so does the demand for water, but at the same time, many rivers are being polluted by industrial chemicals, runoff containing high levels of chemicals from artificial

▲ Crops such as sorghum—being tended here by a farmer in Ethiopia—are more resistant to arid conditions and help the populations of drought-stricken areas survive.

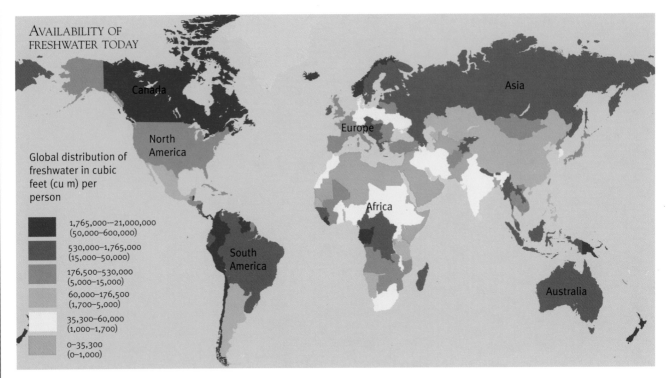

AVAILABILITY OF FRESHWATER TODAY

Global distribution of freshwater in cubic feet (cu m) per person

- 1,765,000–21,000,000 (50,000–600,000)
- 530,000–1,765,000 (15,000–50,000)
- 176,500–530,000 (5,000–15,000)
- 60,000–176,500 (1,700–5,000)
- 35,300–60,000 (1,000–1,700)
- 0–35,300 (0–1,000)

Canada

North America

South America

Europe

Asia

Africa

Australia

▲ The amount of freshwater across the globe is sufficient to supply the world population. However, because it is not evenly distributed, some areas have more freshwater than the population needs, while others suffer a severe lack of it. The worst-hit areas are parts of North Africa; Canada, on the other hand, has more freshwater than it needs for its population.

fertilizers, and domestic sewage. This pollution reduces the levels of fresh, clean water available in many places around the world.

Approximately one-tenth of the world's groundwater supplies are easy to reach, and much of this is being tapped by countries to fulfill their demands for water. Wells and bore holes are sunk deep into the ground to pump supplies of groundwater to the surface. On average, 40 percent of the U.S. population gets its water directly from underground sources across the country. Globally, more than 1.5 billion people rely on groundwater supplies for their drinking water. However, groundwater levels can take a long time to replenish and become exhausted if used at a rapid rate.

Ancient communities in dry climates learned to conserve water and treat it as a precious commodity. The enormous rise in the world's population and the demands on water from industry and intensive agriculture have placed far greater strain on water resources and have increased the importance of water conservation, particularly during drought periods. Water saved by one household or village may be enough to protect the critical needs of others. Water rationing can also be employed in towns and cities to alleviate emergency situations.

Desalination plants solve part of the problem of the lack of freshwater in areas such as the Middle East. At plants like this one in Oman, seawater is processed to remove the salt so it can be used for agricultural and domestic purposes.

Many settlements, such as this one in Cambodia, have been built around floodplains, where farmers can earn a living from the soil.

Why do so many people live in flood-threatened regions?

Floods can bring huge benefits to people. They can supply crucial water and fertile sediments to farmlands. Floods from the Himalaya mountain range, for example, deposit natural phosphates and nitrates in northern India and Bangladesh, which help to enrich the soil. Over thousands of years, sediment deposited by floods has created rich farmlands that now house a large proportion of the world's population. People have been drawn to these areas because of the flat and fertile land, which is suitable for building and provides a prosperous farming environment. Similarly, many of the world's major towns and cities are situated on or near the coast for trading purposes or fishing. Some of these settlements are in areas at risk of coastal flooding.

▶ In parts of Indonesia and China, terraces are built in the sides of hills to prevent soil erosion. Water is retained in the ground by the series of steps; this means that soil is not washed down the slope by rains.

Can flooding be controlled?

Several techniques are used to prevent floods or to control and reduce their harmful impact. Levees are embankments built on either side of a river. These can prevent smaller-scale floods from occurring, but they can force flooding to occur elsewhere on the river system. If levees break, widespread flooding can occur.

Reservoirs and dams help control the flow of water in a region that is likely to flood. In the U.S., the Tennessee Valley Authority (TVA) uses a system of reservoirs and 34 dams to control flooding. Before a potential flood season, the TVA lowers the level of water stored in the reservoirs so they can safely hold high levels of surface runoff. This stored runoff is later released at a controlled rate.

In Egypt, the Aswan High Dam, which stretches across the Nile River, was completed in 1971. The dam has effectively stopped the river's annual floods by trapping its waters in a reservoir and then slowly releasing them during the dry season. However, flood control can come at a price. The farmers on the Nile have been deprived of the fertile, nutrient-rich sediment that the river's seasonal flooding used to bring. The soil in some areas is in danger of containing too much salt, which means that crops cannot grow properly, while erosion and high artificial fertilizer use create further problems for soil quality.

 **Borsha and bonna floods in Bangladesh**

In areas where seasonal or cyclical flooding occurs, people live a precarious existence. They rely on flooding and channel much of its waters for farming, yet a severe flood can be disastrous. Eighty percent of the Asian nation of Bangladesh consists of low-lying floodplains formed by two very large rivers—the Ganges and the Brahmaputra. The people of Bangladesh distinguish between regular floods, called borsha, and larger-than-usual floods, called bonna. Bonna floods are frequently disastrous; in 1988, more than 2,300 people drowned or died of disease spread by floodwaters. Ten years later, another bonna flood covered about 66 percent of the country, leaving more than 20 million homeless.

◀ The Aswan Dam built across the Nile River has created a giant 300-mile-long (480 km) reservoir called Lake Nasser. The dam is part of a project to create large amounts of electricity from the moving waters of the river. It has also controlled annual flooding.

Flood control has also been exerted in coastal regions. Following the disastrous flooding from a coastal storm surge in 1953, the Netherlands began the Delta Plan in 1958 (it was completed in 1985). This huge project includes a series of giant dams on three river deltas, as well as the giant Stormvloedkering. This is a huge storm-surge barrier, 5.5 miles (9 km) long, capable of withstanding more than 33,000 tons (30,000 t) of force from the sea. It is only lowered once a year for testing purposes or when a sea flood is imminent. At other times, it remains open, allowing sea tides to flow. In London, the Thames Barrier protects the capital from the river flooding its banks—it is the largest moveable flood barrier in the world, spanning 1,700 feet (520 m).

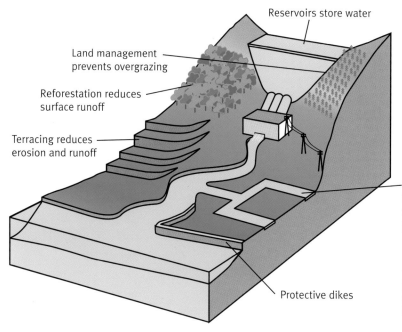

Reservoirs store water

Land management prevents overgrazing

Reforestation reduces surface runoff

Terracing reduces erosion and runoff

Water is channeled into reservoirs through irrigation projects

Protective dikes

◀ There are many measures that can be taken to protect both land and people from the damaging effects of flooding, including reforestation and irrigation projects such as terracing.

▲ This storm-surge barrier, called Stormvloedkering, was built in the Netherlands as part of a project to prevent damage from flooding in the delta areas. This barrier and three huge dams were built between 1958 and 1985.

Is it possible to predict droughts and floods?

New technologies have made it easier to predict where and when floods may strike. Scientists create flood forecasts and issue warnings based on large amounts of data on rainfall or details of a river system and its surrounding area. This data is entered into computer systems to create a

🌐 The 1993 Mississippi flood

The Mississippi-Missouri river system drains more than a quarter of the U.S. and has seen major flooding on a number of occasions. In 1993, torrential rainfall began in April and continued into July. The 1,800-mile (3,000 km) system of levees along the Mississippi could not hold the water, and the river burst its banks, flooding more than 35,000 square miles (90,000 sq km) of land and causing more than $10 billion of damage.

▶ An aerial view of farmland flooded by the Mississippi River in 1993.

model for the region. Warnings of major floods allow the evacuation of people from a threatened region, especially in wealthier countries with highly developed communications and transportation links. Yet many local floods in wealthy countries and larger floods in poorer countries still lead to great destruction and loss of life.

Droughts are much more difficult to predict, as they are longer-term events and occur more gradually—they are not as easy to "spot" as, for example, a hurricane. Because they can strike a far larger area than floods, it is almost impossible to evacuate people from the threatened region. However, with advances in climate modeling, it may be possible to make more accurate predictions of where droughts might strike in the future. This would enable preventive action to be taken and relief and aid to reach an area more swiftly and effectively.

Future advances in weather forecasting technology and greater knowledge about the cycles and processes that shape Earth and its climate may lead to breakthroughs in predicting droughts or floods. In the meantime, both hazards remain a threat to ways of life all over our planet.

▼ Floods in Pennsylvania in 1972. Although recent advances in technology and improved understanding of weather patterns have resulted in better preparation for and responses to such emergencies, flooding remains a serious threat to human life and property.

Glossary

air pressure The force exerted on Earth by the weight of the air above it. Areas of high air pressure usually have warm, dry weather in summer and cold, dry weather in winter. Low pressure areas have more clouds and rain.

aquifer A sideways channel through which groundwater runs beneath the earth.

arid Very dry.

atmosphere The layers of gases, liquids, and solid particles that surround Earth.

blocking high An area of high air pressure that remains stationary, creating low pressure areas around it, resulting in drought conditions.

climate The long-term weather conditions in a particular region.

cloudburst flood A type of flash flood caused by sudden and intense rainfall.

condensation The change from water vapor to liquid water that occurs when air is cooled.

contaminate To poison a water supply with harmful bacteria or chemicals.

continental drought region An area far inland that experiences little or no rainfall, usually caused by the rain shadow effect.

deflation The removal of soil from dry lands by strong winds.

deforestation The cutting down of trees and clearing away of forest areas.

delta The often triangular-shaped alluvial deposition area at the mouth of a river.

desalination The process of removing salt from seawater so it can be used for agricultural and domestic purposes.

desertification The process of expansion and spreading of a desert area, reducing the land's ability to support life.

discharge The volume of water flowing down a river.

drainage basin The area of land into which water from runoff, streams, and tributaries feeds.

drought A period of lower than average rainfall that is long enough to cause hardship to people, plants, and animals.

earthquake Shaking felt at Earth's surface, caused by the movement of Earth's plates pulling apart, pushing together, or grinding alongside one another.

El Niño The name given to the weather conditions associated with the sudden reversal of ocean currents in the Pacific Ocean.

equator An imaginary line that runs around the middle of Earth at an equal distance from the North and South Poles.

erosion The movement or removal of material from a landscape.

evaporation The process by which a liquid, such as water, is changed into a gas when it is heated.

evapotranspiration The loss of water from the planet's surface to the atmosphere through evaporation and transpiration combined.

famine An extended period in which a country or region suffers from a severe shortage of food; famines are often a consequence of drought.

fertile Capable of growing and sustaining plant life or supporting farming.

flash flood A sudden flood that occurs shortly after or during heavy rainfall.

flood When a body of water, such as an ocean or river, rises and overflows onto the surrounding land.

floodplain A flat, low-lying area near a river or stream that is subject to flooding.

fossil fuels Materials that can be burned to generate energy; they are formed from living material that has decayed and was buried in the ground millions of years ago.

global warming The warming of Earth's climate due to an increase in greenhouse gases trapped in the atmosphere.

greenhouse effect The rise in Earth's temperature caused by increasing levels of greenhouse gases being trapped in Earth's atmosphere.

greenhouse gas One of the gases present in Earth's atmosphere—such as carbon dioxide, methane, or nitrous oxide—that warms the planet.

groundwater Water stored in underground rocks.

humidity The amount of water vapor in the air.

hurricane A tropical storm that contains fast-moving, spiraling winds.

ice jam When parts of a frozen river melt at different rates, causing melted water to be blocked by ice and unable to flow, leading to flooding.

impermeable Unable to absorb water easily.

infiltration The movement of water from ground surface to soil.

infrastructure Basic facilities and structures in countries or settlements, such as transportation and communications links and water and power supplies.

irrigation Artificial watering of the land in which people use technology to allow crops to grow.

landslide The rapid movement of soil and rock material down a slope.

latitude A region's distance from the equator, measured in degrees north or south.

levee An embankment—generally constructed close to the banks of a river, stream, or lake—intended to protect the surrounding land from flooding.

meandering The looping and winding of a river within its floodplain.

mineral A chemical substance in Earth's crust.

monsoon A seasonal shift in winds over large areas of land, caused by a dramatic change in temperature.

permeable Able to absorb water easily.

precipitation The various forms of water—rain, snow, sleet, and hail—that fall to Earth's surface.

rain shadow area An area on the sheltered side of a mountain range that receives low levels of rainfall.

rapids Fast-flowing parts of a river.

reservoir An artificial lake, often contained by a dam, used to generate a water supply or control the amount of water in a river to help prevent floods or droughts.

runoff The part of rainfall that reaches streams or rivers; the remainder either evaporates into the atmosphere or seeps below ground.

saturated A condition of a material, such as soil, when it cannot absorb any more water.

sediment The solid that settles at the bottom of a liquid.

silt Very fine soil particles deposited by rivers.

soil erosion The process by which loose soil is washed or blown away.

soluble Capable of being dissolved.

source The place where a stream or river begins to flow.

spring tide A tide that is higher than normal, which occurs when the sun and the moon are aligned and are both exerting a strong gravitational force on Earth's water.

stomata The "pores" found on the underside of leaves on plants and trees, through which water is transpired.

storm surge An abnormal rise in sea level, usually caused by an area of low pressure over a body of water, that can be responsible for coastal flooding.

subsidence The sinking of land.

terracing The process of cutting steep steps in the side of a slope or hill to prevent fertile topsoil from being washed away.

tide A regular movement of seawater toward and away from the land; caused by the gravity exerted by the sun and moon on Earth.

topsoil The fertile upper layer of soil, in which plants and crops grow best.

transpiration The process by which plants release water vapor into the atmosphere through openings in their leaves.

tributary A stream or other body of water that contributes to another body of water.

tsunami A giant ocean wave—often called a tidal wave—caused by an undersea earthquake, volcanic eruption, or landslide.

volcano A crack in Earth's crust through which molten rock and lava erupts.

water cycle The constant and repeated movement of water between the air, land, and sea.

water table The upper level of saturated soil or rock.

Further Information

Books

Burt, Christopher C. *Extreme Weather: A Guide & Record Book*. New York: W. W. Norton, 2004.

Chambers, Catherine. *Drought*. Chicago: Heinemann Library, 2001.

Engelbert, Phillis. *Dangerous Planet: The Science of Natural Disasters*. Detroit: UXL, 2001.

Gifford, Clive. *The Kingfisher Geography Encyclopedia*. Boston: Kingfisher, 2003.

Green, Mary. *Rivers in Action*. North Mankato, Minn.: Smart Apple Media, 2005.

Web sites

http://www.dartmouth.edu/~floods/
The home page of the Dartmouth Flood Observatory, which contains analyses of flood events around the world using satellite images featured on the Web site.

http://www.drought.noaa.gov/
The National Oceanic and Atmospheric Administration's (NOAA) drought information center, which includes information on drought and climate conditions.

http://www.redcross.org/services/disaster/
Fact sheets from the American Red Cross on water conservation and how to survive disasters.

http://www.unicef.org/drought/
Updated accounts of drought disasters facing many countries around the world.

http://www.usgs.gov/
The home page of the U.S. Geological Survey, with resources and news stories about the geography and geology of the U.S.

Index

Acknowledgements

Picture Credits

Cover: (t) Grunewald Olivier/OSF **(bl)** Ted Mead/OSF
(br) Mauro Fermariello/Science Photo Library **6(t)** NASA/OSF
6(b) Paul Nevin/OSF **7** Jean-Leo Dugast/Still Pictures
9(t) Stephen J. Krasemann/Science Photo Library **9(b)** VVG/
Science Photo Library **10(b)** © Pablo Corral V/Corbis
11(b) Emmanuel Jeanjean/ Still Pictures **12** 2002 Orbital Imaging
Corporation/Science Photo Library **13(l)** Grunewald Olivier/
OSF **14(l)** © Gallo Images/Corbis **14(r)** Ted Mead/OSF
15(b) C. Allen Morgan/Still Pictures **16** C.K.Au/UNEP/ Still
Pictures **17(b)** Earth Satellite Corporation/Science Photo Library
19(t) UNEP/Still Pictures **19(b)** Argus/ Still Pictures **20** Jim
Reed/Science Photo Library **21(t)** Eco **21(b)** © Bettman/Corbis
22(t) Mauro Fermariello/Science Photo Library **22(b)** Per-
Anders Petersson/UNEP/Still Pictures **23(t)** © Jayanta Shaw/
Reuters/Corbis **23(b)** © Marc Serota/Reuters/Corbis **24(t)** © Tim
Thompson/Corbis **25(t)** © Stringer/Malaysia/Reuters/Corbis
25(b) © Keith Dannemiller/Corbis **26(t)** © Royalty-free/Corbis
27 David McNew/Still Pictures **28(t)** © Reuters/Corbis
28(b) Frans Lemmens/Still Pictures **29** Mike Boyatt/ Agstock/
Science Photo Library **30(t)** Kevin Lane/UNEP/Still Pictures
31 Nigel Dickinson/Still Pictures **32(t)** Mark Edwards/Still
Pictures **32(b)** Kittprempool-UNEP/Still Pictures **33(t)** Eco
33(b) Voltchev/UNEP/Still Pictures **34** © Gary Braasch/ Corbis
35(t) © Bettmann/Corbis **35(b)** Pieternella Pieterse/Still Pictures
37(t) Bojan Brecelj/Still Pictures **37(b)** © Kevin R. Morris/Corbis
38 Friedrich Stark/Still Pictures **39(t)** Jorgen Schytte/Still
Pictures **40(t)** © Cees Van Leeuwen; Cordaly Photo Library Ltd/
Corbis **40(b)** © Andrew Holbrooke/Corbis **41** © Bettmann/Corbis